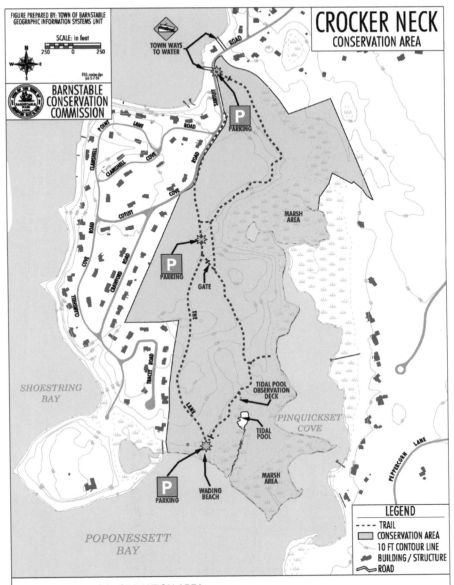

CROCKER NECK
CONSERVATION AREA

FIGURE PREPARED BY: TOWN OF BARNSTABLE
GEOGRAPHIC INFORMATION SYSTEMS UNIT

SCALE: in feet

250   0   250

FILE: crocker.apr
Jan 5-7-94

BARNSTABLE CONSERVATION COMMISSION

TOWN WAYS TO WATER

P PARKING

P PARKING

GATE

P PARKING

WADING BEACH

MARSH AREA

TIDAL POOL OBSERVATION DECK

TIDAL POOL

PINQUICKSET COVE

MARSH AREA

SHOESTRING BAY

POPONESSETT BAY

PEPPERCORN LANE

LEGEND
- - - - TRAIL
▢ CONSERVATION AREA
— 10 FT CONTOUR LINE
BUILDING / STRUCTURE
ROAD

CROCKER NECK CONSERVATION AREA

DIRECTIONS: From Cotuit Center, go west on School Street, 4/10 mile and turn left onto Crocker Neck Road. Crocker Neck Road ends at Santuit Road without a stop sign. Follow Santuit road south. The north gate trailhead parking area is 1 mile from the beginning of Crocker Neck Road and is on the left side of the road. There is limited parking here. Additional parking is just down the road. Look for the Crocker Neck Conservation Area sign. Drive down the dirt road (The Lane) and you will see a small parking area on the right. Beach access is at the end of The Lane.

SITE DESCRIPTION: Crocker Neck, encompassing 97 acres, is a very peaceful area with an observation deck overlooking Pinquickset Cove. You will find a beautiful interpretive trail meandering along an old dike, crossing a coastal bank, passing through a quiet pir... wetland and terminating at the shore. Waterfowl hunting is the only h... to the current rules and regulations. Check the kiosks at the trailhea... information.

This map provided by the Barnstable

D1314772

Published by Gilbert Newton
gdnewton@comcast.net • www.capecodcoastalecology.net
to benefit the Barnstable Land Trust

ISBN 978-0-9816873-8-4

To purchase a copy of this book, contact:
Barnstable Land Trust
407 North Street, Hyannis, Massachusetts 02601
508-771-2585 • www.BLT.org

Cover photograph of a kingfisher by Chris Dumas

The Ecology of

A Cape Cod Salt Marsh

A Tour through Crocker Neck

by Gilbert Newton

with photography
by Chris Dumas

To the

Residents of the Town of Barnstable, Massachusetts

who had the wisdom

to preserve and protect

this valuable resource.

Table Of Contents

Introduction

It's hard to know how a community feels about a piece of land until it is threatened by development.

In 1985, I had just begun working for the Barnstable Land Trust. Two years before that, the Town's Conservation Commission, under the leadership of Gil Newton, had created the first comprehensive Open Space Plan for Barnstable. In the process, they had engaged the community to think about important parcels worthy of protection and that attracted the attention of political leaders. The Selectmen – Marty Flynn, Jeff Wilson and John Klimm (now Town Manager) – followed up by appointing an Open Space Task Force, which asked for village participation to identify priority parcels for acquisition. A wave of open space preservation was underway. I came in on the crest of that wave.

Crocker Neck juts out into Popponesset Bay; the Bay is the political boundary between the Towns of Barnstable and Mashpee. In Barnstable it is often referred to as the "Forgotten Bay" because it is shallow and far from the hustle and bustle of Hyannis. Surrounded by water on two sides, Crocker Neck is isolated, wild and rich. All manner of wildlife inhabit its upland forest and its wetland fringes.

When developers proposed to cluster 18 homes all along the water's edge, the community was outraged and they mobilized. With the Open Space Task Force in place, there was a growing movement to bring vital parcels throughout the Town to the voters for approval. Selectman Klimm suggested that we find a way to purchase the property from the developers. And so it happened that the developers agreed to sell the land to the Town to be held under the jurisdiction of the Conservation Commission.

In November of 1985, Town Meeting authorized the preservation of 492 acres with a price tag of 17.1 million dollars, subject to voter approval. In December, the town-wide initiative was over-whelmingly supported when voters went to the polls to raise their property taxes for a period of 20 years in order to pay for the land. Crocker Neck was saved!

Land to the north of Crocker Neck was already held in conservation by the Town. An additional 15 acres to the west was transferred to the jurisdiction of the Conservation Commission. Today, the Crocker Neck Conservation Area is 97 acres of protected land, laced with paths for humans and wildlife.

We are lucky to live in a community where people are passionate about their surroundings. And we are privileged to have Gil Newton in our midst. Gil has lived his life in Cotuit and taught scores of Cape Cod kids and young adults about the mysteries of the natural world.

And now, 25 years later, Gil has given each of us a tool to guide us through the Crocker Neck Conservation Area. In the process, he has graciously donated the profits of this book to the Barnstable Land Trust so they can do more to protect the open spaces and special places of our community. We are grateful for his generosity and support.

Enjoy!

> Jaci Barton
> Cotuit Resident and
> Executive Director of Barnstable Land Trust

Preface

Like so many before me, I am attracted to wild, open spaces that enchant and enrich. I find a sense of renewal and connection to these natural areas as places of solitude, surrounded by scenery and wildlife. Open spaces, such as forests, meadows, and beaches sustain the existence of a land ethic which can be passed on to generation after generation. We all have those special places that upgrade our lives into a meaningful existence.

Crocker Neck is such a place to me. Located in Cotuit, Massachusetts, it is a 97 acre parcel of conservation land owned and maintained by the Town of Barnstable. Thirty-five acres of upland surrounding the marsh was purchased in 1985 for three million dollars. I remember it well. I was the chairman of the Barnstable Conservation Commission at that time. This board was the architect of the Open Space Plan that included Crocker Neck. I participated in all of the hearings and campaigns that led to its acquisition.

I walked the site many times before its purchase and continue to explore and enjoy it today. It is one of the more popular field trip destinies for my students at the Cape Cod Community College.

The salt marsh at Crocker Neck is a complex system rich in resources and beauty. From the diverse woodland leading to the marsh to the extensive salt-tolerant plants by the water, this land is home to many species of coastal wildlife. Some spend a small portion of their lives here while others make it their permanent residence. Some species, particularly birds, are only temporary visitors, but the marsh helps sustain their seasonal journeys.

This guide is an introduction to this very special place. Open to the public for walking, its trails and pathways represent a cross-section of woodland and marine habitats on Cape Cod. The ecology of this area is what interests me the most, hence the focus of this book. There is a close interdependence between all the living organisms in this fascinating ecosystem. This is a place for exploration and discovery in all seasons and all weather conditions. Welcome to the Crocker Neck Conservation Area. I hope your visit is as rewarding to you as it has been to me.

The Values of a Salt Marsh

There are many kinds of wetlands depending on the type of vegetation and soil, the proximity to the water table, and the animal inhabitants. Different plants and animals have adapted to varying environmental conditions, and may occupy a specific section of an ecosystem.

One of the most important wetland systems is the salt marsh. These ecologically significant ecosystems are formed in quiet bays and estuaries where their grasses trap sediment with each incoming tide. These semi-aquatic barriers act as buffers, protecting upland areas from erosion, and the aquifer from salt water intrusion. Even during a powerful hurricane, a salt marsh can withstand the battering of waves and wind, and can reduce flooding by absorbing coastal waters like a giant sponge.

Salt marshes are important nurseries for large populations of commercially important finfish and shellfish. Also, there is a high biodiversity of other species, the more common ones described in this book. Though some animals spend their life cycle in a marsh, many others are visitors at different times of the year. Some have their young in a marsh, seeking protection in the creeks from predators and the harsh physical conditions of the open ocean. Some migrate through at high tide, feeding on the rich, decomposing plant material called detritus. Certain bird species find refuge in a marsh, and a resting place from their long migratory routes. Even terrestrial animals, such as raccoons, can be seen foraging and feeding on small crustaceans in the transition zone between forest and marsh.

The plant life is particularly interesting in this system because it is so essential to the food web. The tall cordgrass and the extensive marsh hay are primary producers, bringing energy into the system through the process of photosynthesis where they convert sunlight and carbon dioxide to sugars and oxygen. Their unique adaptations to this environment are described in the guide.

The muddy sediments should not be ignored as one explores a marsh. Microscopic algae, bacteria, and nematode worms play a major role in this elaborate movement of energy from tiny critters all the way up the food web to the large fish in the system. Many of these microscopic forms photosynthesize as well, while others are important decomposers, breaking apart the large mats of decaying cordgrass to be used as food for a diverse number of species.

One interesting relationship between plant and animal can be seen at low tide along the banks of the marsh. Embedded in the peat are large clumps of ribbed mussels. These animals can withstand periods of exposure between tides, but they are often given added protection by the rockweed which grows over the mussels. The rockweed provides a kind of canopy along the edges of the marsh, and its tissues retain moisture at low tide. Many small animal species seek shelter under the rockweed, while others attach their eggs. At high tide the rockweed also protects these animals from any strong wave action. Ultimately, the rockweed also contributes to the food web through photo-synthesis and the formation of detritus.

Salt marshes also have the ability to filter some pollutants from groundwater, particularly nutrients like nitrogen, thus protecting nearby estuaries from algae population blooms and subsequent mollusk and fish kills. There are some communities that have taken advantage of this ability and use marshes as natural filters of wastewater. The nutrients are trapped and used by the marsh grasses. Consequently, the amount of nutrients entering the bay is reduced.

Salt marsh conservation is important in maintaining a healthy coastline. Many salt marsh systems are currently being restored by increasing the tidal flow. This has also reduced the spread of the invasive plant *Phragmites* which is highly competitive with

other species. Unfortunately, salt marshes continue to degrade in many areas because of the pressures of increased population growth, such as development in the watershed. Incremental losses of open space can also adversely affect marshes. Still, there is an increased awareness by the public that these ecosystems must be protected for future generations.

Around the Marsh

Many salt marshes are surrounded by small transitional woodland habitats. Certain plant species have evolved adaptations to survive exposure to the ocean side. The pitch pine (*Pinus rigida*) is characterized by three needles, about three to five inches long, in each bundle or fascicle. The large female cones are prickly, and are one to three inches long. The smaller male cones are in clumps and release an enormous amount of yellow pollen in the spring. The pitch pine is a hardy species and can survive salt spray as well as the sandy soil in this area. Tall pitch pines in the woods produce needles in the canopy only in order to capture enough sunlight for photosynthesis.

A taller pine that grows further from the marsh is the white pine (*Pinus strobus*). This tree can easily be distinguished from the pitch pine. The needles are soft with a bluish-green tinge, and are in bundles of five, compared to the three in the pitch pine. The white pine is home to many birds and squirrels. Its wood has been commercially important for the construction of homes and ships. The white pines in this area are mixed in with the dominant deciduous oak trees.

A common coniferous tree that is often seen growing in rows is the Eastern red cedar (*Juniperus virginianum*). This is a medium-sized tree that grows 20 to 40 feet high. Its branches have scale-like leaves and may contain numerous blue berries, which are actually cones, each with one to two seeds. These berries are consumed by many bird species which pass the seeds through their digestive system, and therefore increase the tree's dispersal. I have observed that some cedars near marshes may be infected by the cedar-apple rust, a fungal gall that results in large drooping, yellowish-orange growths on the branches. These fungi may occur after several rainy days, and can spread from tree to tree.

Along the edge of this forest and leading into the marsh is a transitional zone that is colonized by several small woodland plants including a variety of moss species. Mosses are non-vascular plants that lack internal tissues for the transport of sugars, minerals, and water. Mosses need water for reproduction so they grow in large beds to conserve water. However, they can also tolerate long periods of dry weather. The plant resembles a small clump of needles in a whorl. Look closely at a moss colony for the tall brown stalks which release the spores from a terminal capsule. Mosses help prepare the soil for other plants to grow in the early stages of forest succession. Like other small plants in the edge habitat, they also help prevent erosion.

Reindeer moss (*Cladonia rangiferana*) also grows in large clumps at the edge of the woods. This plant is actually a lichen and not a moss. It's one of the fruticose lichens and is an example of a symbiotic relationship between an alga and a fungus. It can survive a wide range of temperatures and is often found in well-drained soils such as the sandy ones here. Reindeer moss is also highly adapted to changes in rainfall. It has a rough texture during times of drought, but becomes softer after it rains. The plant grows as large mats on the forest ground.

Growing with the mosses and lichens is a small, evergreen plant with shiny green leaves and red berries. This has several common names including wintergreen, teaberry, and checkerberry (*Gaultheria procumbens*). Small, white, bell-shaped flowers appear in the summer followed by the formation of red fruits. Tear one of the leaves and smell the slight wintergreen odor. This edge habitat plant also protects the soil from eroding. The berries provide a food source for birds and small animals.

Another small, bright green plant in this environment is bearberry (*Arctostaphylus uva-ursi*). This early colonizing plant has small white flowers shaped like a cup, and is another plant with red berries that are popular with birds. The leaves are evergreen so, like the others, this is an effective groundcover for preventing erosion. Also adapted to the sandy soil, its thick leaves help prevent water loss.

Plants of the Marsh

There are several vascular and non-vascular plants in a salt marsh. The seaweeds, or marine algae, are technically not plants, but are included in the kingdom Protista. One common green alga (shown below) is green fleece (*Codium fragile*), also called dead man's fingers. Codium was introduced into this area many years ago. It has since established itself as a major nuisance, particularly in sensitive areas like estuaries. Here it can be a pest by attaching to the shells of oysters, scallops, and slipper snails. It weighs them down, removes them from their native habitats by floating, and sometimes covers their filter-feeding siphons. This alga has a spongy texture, and its branches have puffy, swollen tips. It can grow up to three feet in length.

Sea lettuce (*Ulva lactuca*) is a common green alga that consists of large sheets often folded along the edges. It consists of two cell layers thick, and can grow up to three feet in length. The presence of large sheets of this alga in a bay or estuary around a marsh could suggest the presence of high concentrations of nitrogen. It is also tolerant to changes in salinity, so you may find some of it in the marsh creeks.

Rockweed (*Fucus vesiculosus*) is a common brown alga growing on the banks of a salt marsh. It attaches its holdfast to a strong substrate, and efficiently provides shelter for some marsh animals, such as ribbed mussels. This alga is characterized by two opposite air bladders which may appear at several locations along the blade. These air bladders enable the alga to float in order to photosynthesize more successfully. Brown in color, the blade also has a distinct midrib. The tips of the alga are swollen when fertile, and these structures release the reproductive cells into the water.

Along the lower part of the salt marsh in the daily tidal flood zone exists a tall, visible grass. Cordgrass (*Spartina alterniflora*) is a perennial plant that grows up to eight feet tall, and is one of the more conspicuous vascular plants in the marsh. In order to survive the exposure to sea water, this plant removes salt through its leaves. Rub your fingers along one of its blades and you can feel the tiny salt crystals. Cordgrass is also important ecologically when it dies and decomposes into large mats. These contribute to other forms of decaying organic material known as detritus, and are removed by the tides to support large populations of animals offshore.

The part of the salt marsh that resembles a large, green meadow is composed mostly of salt marsh hay (*Spartina patens*). Unlike the cordgrass, this plant is flooded irregularly during spring tides and storm surges. Salt marsh hay grows up to three feet in height and often appears as large mats in the upper portions of the marsh. It is a major habitat for many animals, including fiddler crabs, marsh snails, and some bivalves or clams. Like the cordgrass, it contributes to the detritus. Historically, it was used for cattle grazing, and as a source of thatch for insulation and roofs.

Surrounding the salt marsh at a slightly higher elevation than the cordgrass is a small deciduous shrub called marsh elder (*Iva frutescens*). This plant grows around three to six feet high, and has toothed opposite leaves. Small white flowers appear in the summer. Though this shrub can survive periodic salt spray and water, it also is adapted to dry conditions. Marsh elder forms a distinct zone, often forming a ring around the upper part of the marsh. It is sometimes confused with the groundsel tree (*Baccharis halimifolia*), except that this plant has alternate leaves instead.

An interesting succulent plant (shown right) called glasswort (*Salicornia europea*), or the sea pickle, can be found growing in the open, muddy areas of the salt marsh. The plants can grow up to a foot long and are characterized by their thick, green, jointed stems. There are small scale-like leaves along the joints. The plant is considered edible, but I find it too salty. At some locations glasswort grows extensively in the upper marsh. The plants are purplish-red in the fall, but dry up as brown stalks in the winter.

A small, but dense, population of black grass (*Juncus gerardi*) can be seen in the upper, less salty, parts of the marsh. This plant grows one to two feet tall, and has thin, green stems. Black grass is a perennial plant. It often colonizes open, muddy sections of the upper marsh. It grows beyond most of the tidal influence, and therefore forms a distinct zone.

Sea Lavender photo by James R. Brown

Around mid-summer clusters of small purple flowers can be seen in the marsh. Upon closer inspection, you will see one of the more popular marsh plants known as sea lavender (*Limonium nashii*). Found in the upper marsh amidst the salt marsh hay, this attractive plant can grow between one and two feet tall. When not in flower, it can be identified by a set of flattened leaves on the ground. Unfortunately, this plant is frequently collected for dry flower arrangements that reduce the population by eliminating a source of seeds. Please don't pick this plant. Enjoy it in its natural habitat.

Another common grass that grows in the upper marsh is spike grass (*Distichlis spicata*). This plant can form dense populations, and spreads by an underground stem called a rhizome. Like cordgrass, it can release salt through its linear leaves. When dead, the leaves tend to curl, distinguishing it from the nearby salt marsh hay. It spreads easily into open areas, and can sometimes be found in small groups near the pannes.

Small daisy-like flowers can be seen in the marsh from late summer to early fall. The salt marsh aster (*Aster tenuifolius*) grows with the salt marsh hay and sea lavender, and has purplish white flowers on a smooth stem. Most of the flower heads I've observed are around half an inch across. Even in winter you can find the dead stalks remaining on the marsh. The leaves are very thin and linear, but it's the flowers that add color to the marsh in the summer.

One unwanted plant is the tall reed (*Phragmites australis*), an eight to fifteen foot tall grass that grows along the edges of salt marshes, and particularly in areas that have been disturbed. Its appearance indicates the presence of freshwater, either ground-water, streams, or runoff. This plant is one of the most invasive

Phragmites photo by Nancy Viall Shoemaker

species in the northeast, and easily spreads with its extensive rhizome. The plant can be identified throughout the year by its terminal brown and feathery head of seeds. Several projects have been implemented to control this invader, but the most success-ful involved increasing the flow of salt water into the area. Some of my students determined that Phragmites can survive, even thrive, in salinities up to 15 parts per thousand. Freshwater is zero, and saltwater averages around 32 parts per thousand.

Another common invasive plant is poison ivy (*Toxicodendron radicans*). All parts of the plant contain urushiol which can cause severe itching if contacted. The plant is easy to identify with its compound leaf of three leaflets, a cluster of small white flowers

Poison Ivy photo by James R. Brown

in early summer, and grayish berries in the fall. However, the habitat of the plant varies considerably. It can extend its aerial roots as a vine, and it can grow as a small shrub close to, and around, the edge of the marsh. The plant is highly adapted to this environment, tolerating sandy soil and salt spray.

Animals around the Marsh

Walk along the banks of the marsh at low tide, and look under the rockweed. Embedded in the banks are large clumps of ribbed mussels (*Modiolus demissus*). These animals (shown below) are attached to the peat and each other by strong byssus threads. These bivalves are cylindrical, and the shells have ridges or ribs along the length, hence their name. The rockweed provides the animals with protection from predators and desiccation at low tide. The mussels are filter-feeders, using their siphons to strain water for small particles of food. This species should not be confused with the edible blue mussel (*Mytilus edulis*) which is more likely found in a rockier habitat.

Quahogs (*Mercenaria mercenaria*) are economically important shellfish that are adapted to the changing salinity in a salt marsh. Their thick shells also have a purple lining on the inside, and can grow up to four inches long. The animal burrows just below the substrate, and filter-feeds with a small siphon that protrudes from the surface. Quahogs can live up to two decades, and the approximate age can be determined by examining the distinct growth rings on the outside of the shell. Native Americans used these shells as a source of currency. Quahogs are still important to the economy as an edible species in the form of littlenecks, cherrystones, and chowder.

Shells of the stout tagelus (*Tagelus plebeius*) are often found in the marsh, and are some-times confused with razor clams. This animal is shorter than the razor clam, and grows to about four inches long. Also, its hinge is located in the middle of the shell. It has a chalky white appearance and texture. These mollusks burrow in the mud about a foot deep.

One familiar shell that you may find in the marsh is the common bay scal-lop (*Aequipecten irradians*). Chances are that the shell washed in with the tides from its regular habitat in the subtidal eel grass beds. These shells are identified by their rough ribs, and grow up to three inches in length. The eel grass provides them with protection because they do not dig under the sand like most clams. Instead, they can escape predators by snapping the two shells together, propelling themselves away. Scallops can live up to two years, but they are an economically important edible species.

The slipper snail (*Crepidula fornicata*) is a common mollusk that is often found washed up on sandy beaches in huge numbers. Many of them can be found in stacks, or attached to other shells, rocks, even *Codium*. They are easily identified by the presence of a small indentation or platform along the opening of the shell. The shell may grow around an inch in size, with the females being slightly larger than the males.

To find a razor clam (*Ensis directus*) in a salt marsh, you need to locate an open, muddy area. These mollusks burrow under the surface of the mud flat, but they use their strong foot to dig very quickly into the substrate. It is more likely that you will find a shell on the surface, which is easy to identify. It's about five times longer than it is wide, and brown along the edges. Don't confuse this with the stout tagelus which is thicker and whiter.

When the tide goes out, take a look in one of the many creeks that cut through the marsh. You are likely to see thousands of small dark snails feeding on the remains of a dead fish or crab. These scavengers of the marsh are the eastern mud snails (*Ilyanassa obsoleta*). Attracted to the decaying organisms, they travel in large numbers to the food source and scrape it with their radula, a kind of tongue-like structure with teeth. They also feed on the numerous phytoplankton or microscopic algae in the sediments. Sometimes the animal's shell (one-half to one inch long) is coated with a layer of algae, giving it a darker appearance in the water.

Shown here is an amazing animal that lives in the upper marsh, known as the salt marsh snail (*Melampus bidentatus*), also called the coffee bean snail. This tiny, light brown snail can be found under the blades of salt marsh hay at low tide. However, the salt marsh snail breathes air, so it must crawl to the top of the grass during flooding to avoid drowning. I've seen dozens of these animals during a storm tide at many salt marshes. I suspect that their populations fluctuate from year to year because some years they are difficult to find. The animals feed on small bits of algae and detritus on the substrate.

The common periwinkle (*Littorina littorea*) is found mainly along a rocky substrate, though it can also live in large numbers in a salt marsh. This tiny snail grows a little over an inch long, and its shell is dark and spiral. The periwinkle feeds mainly on microscopic algae that it scrapes from plants and rocks with its radula. This animal can live for long periods of time

outside the water. I have seen large populations of them embedded in the peat in the upper marsh, and many more feeding on the marsh surface.

One of the most abundant and ecologically important animals in a salt marsh is the fiddler crab (*Uca* species). These animals are active at low tide during the warm months, and are often seen emerging from their burrows in large numbers. Their carapace is one to two inches long, and their eyes are on long stalks. The males have one large claw which is used in courtship and defense. The animals feed on bits of decaying organic matter, but also contribute to the food web as a source of nutrition for birds and larger crabs. For the environment they aerate the sediments with their digging, and fertilize the marsh with their wastes.

An abundant and easily observable animal is the green crab (*Carcinus maenus*), found mainly in the intertidal zone. Look under rocks and by jetties to find this common species. This introduced crab can also survive the changing salinity of the marsh. These crabs can swim, but have pointed hind legs rather than the paddle-shaped ones seen in blue crabs. Green crabs grow up to three inches long, and feed on other animals in the substrate such as clams and worms.

The blue crab (*Callinectes sapidus*) is a common edible species living in the bay around the marsh. This is an easy crab to identify  with its blue shell or carapace, paddle-shaped hind legs, and sharp spines on the edges of its shell. Because of its aggressive pinch, it is one crab that must be handled with care. The blue crab is a commercially important species, and can breed in large numbers. It feeds on other crabs and clams, and is an important food source for birds. These animals grow by molting, the shedding of their shell. They also have a strong ability to regenerate lost claws.

The spider crab (*Libinia emarginata*) is one of the most common animals in the estuary or bay surrounding the marsh. Its brown, spiny carapace helps it camouflage against the muddy bottom. The animal grows to about four inches in length, but its legs can extend up to a foot. This  crab is harmless, and feeds mainly on bits of organic material in the water and sediments. One of its unique characteristics is that it actively attaches algae and small animals to its carapace, giving it the appearance of a tiny marine zoo crawling on the bottom of the bay. You often find just the remains of this animal as seen here.

Along the muddy banks of the marsh are large burrows, the homes of the elusive marsh crab (*Sesarma reticulatum*). This animal has a blackish square carapace, and feeds mainly on the nearby cordgrass. At low tide you can observe many opportunistic fiddler crabs in the burrows, but they need to be careful as the marsh crab has been known to feed on them as well. On field trips I usually refer to this part of the marsh as the "crab condos."

In the muddy creeks where there are thousands of mud snails you can occasionally observe one of the "snails" moving a lot faster than the others. Scoop this one up with a net and you will discover a tiny hermit crab (*Pagurus longicarpus*) has taken up residence in the shell. If you hold it quietly in your hand, it will emerge and you might observe its large right claw. Hermit crabs must change shells as they grow, though this species doesn't grow much more than a half-inch long. It also attracts the growth of a small hydroid known as snail fur (*Hydractinia echinata*) on the shell.

One of the most important animals found in bays and estuaries is the horseshoe crab (*Limulus polyphemus*), a primitive relative of spiders and scorpions. Its name derives from its shape, and can be recognized by its long tail or caudal spine, and a large pair of compound eyes on its carapace. The adult females can grow up to two feet, and lay thousands of eggs in the spring which are then fertilized by the male and often consumed by hungry migratory shore birds. Horseshoe crabs molt from the head first, unlike true crabs which molt from the tail end. They feed on mollusks and worms, and are harmless to humans. In fact, a substance in their blue blood will clot in the presence of bacterial toxins. This substance is widely used in medical facilities to test for these poisons. A horseshoe crab carapace may contain many hitchhiking organisms, including algae, small mollusks, and barnacles.

When the tide recedes, many parts of the marsh get exposed as mud flats. It is in these microhabitats that various species of worms can be found. Certainly one of the largest and most conspicuous is the carnivorous clam worm (*Nereis virens*). Growing over a foot long, these reddish-brown segmented worms live under rocks and in burrows. They emerge at night to hunt other worms and mollusks with their strong jaws. Though commonly used as fish bait, they can bite when handled.

Scattered throughout the salt marsh are small, shallow pools of water called pannes. Though these areas have very muddy substrates, they also may be inhabited by tiny glass shrimp (*Palaemonetes spp.*). Their clear bodies are an energy source for larger animals in the marsh food web. They, in turn, feed on the smaller animals and plankton in the marsh sediments. Using a hand lens, the shrimp can be identified by the presence of claws on the first two pairs of legs.

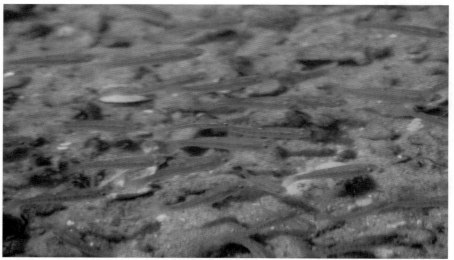

The mummichog (*Fundulus heteroclitus*), also called the killifish, can be seen (above) swimming in large schools in the muddy creeks of the marsh. This small fish ranges from three to five inches long. It usually moves in with the tides, though several can get trapped in the marsh creeks and pannes at low tide. It feeds on a wide variety of sources, including algae, shrimp, and mollusks. This greenish fish has one dorsal fin and a round caudal fin. They can tolerate rapid changes in salinity and oxygen levels that occur regularly due to tidal change and freshwater runoff.

Rock barnacles (*Semibalanus balanoides*) are more frequently found on rocks in the intertidal zone. However, they can be seen in a salt marsh attached to other animals, such as horseshoe crabs or spider crabs. Like many other invertebrates, the larval stage of this crustacean is part of the plankton. Still after it settles on a surface, the adult can grow up to one inch long. These animals are filter-feeders, using their tiny feet to capture plankton while waving through the water. If they are attached to a moving crab, they get transported to various locations where food is available. Barnacles can also form distinct bands or zones along a jetty or piling and are often found near a population of rockweed.

In addition to the plant poison ivy, there is an animal to avoid, namely the deer tick (*Ixodes scapularis*). This tiny arachnid can carry the bacterium that causes Lyme disease. You should always check yourself after visiting the salt marsh as this disease can lead to serious medical problems. The deer tick's nymph stage is particularly infectious and occurs in late spring to early summer. This animal is mainly found in the tall grasses surrounding the marsh.

Don't confuse this animal with the larger dog or wood tick (*Dermacentor variabilis*) which is also found in grassy habitats. This animal can transmit the disease Rocky Mountain spotted fever, but does not transmit Lyme disease.

Drawing by Chris Dumas

One animal which you may not want to encounter is the greenhead fly (*Tabanus americanus*). About an inch long, these insects yield a painful bite. It is the female fly that attacks because she needs a blood meal for her eggs. Once hatched, the maggots will spend the winter in the mud feeding on other small animals.

They emerge around July as the pesky fly, and can be identified by their green head, not to mention their aggressive behavior. The blue boxes you see in the summer are greenhead fly traps. The flies are attracted to the color, and cannot escape once inside the box. Though these animals are a nuisance to humans, they are an important food source for many birds, such as swallows.

Many salt marshes in this area exhibit long, straight ditches which were dug to control the populations of the salt marsh mosquito (*Aedes sollicitans*). The increased flow of water allowed predators, such as the mummichogs, to enter and feed on the larval stages of the animal. The standing water is a perfect habitat for the insects to lay their eggs and go through their life cycle. The adult female needs blood from a mammal for her eggs, thus being a pest to visiting humans. Still, it's important to remember that these insects, as well as others, are important to the overall food web of the marsh.

The osprey (*Pandion heliaetus*) is a magnificent bird of prey that lives in a large nest at the top of a tall tree or pole constructed to increase their population. The bird (above) has a bend in its wings and a wingspan of around five feet long. It can be identified by its white head with a black mark across the eyes, looking like a mask. An excellent fisherman, an osprey often is seen hovering high in the air before it plunges to the water and emerges with a fish trapped in its talons. Since the pesticide DDT was banned in the United States, the osprey has made a remarkable comeback from the brink of extinction.

The snowy egret (*Egretta thula*) is a common marsh bird that often feeds in the creeks on the crustaceans and mummichogs. I usually see several egrets feeding together. The bird is around two feet tall, and has white feathers, black legs, and yellow feet. There is also a characteristic yellow mark around the eyes. Use the binoculars again to help you distinguish these birds from other, less common species.

The green-backed heron (*Butorides virescens*) can usually be spotted around dusk, quietly sitting along the edge of the marsh creek. The bird appears to be crouching because its neck is tightly pulled in. The adult heron is a little over a foot long. It has a greenish cap on its head and long yellow legs. Its body is dark green, and is often hiding by the tall grasses where it sits. The green-backed heron feeds on small animals such as crabs, fish, and insects in the marsh.

Photograph of green-backed heron by Elliott Carr

The great blue heron (*Ardea herodias*) is an unmistakable bird which is often seen in a marsh feeding on the plentiful fish in the creeks and surrounding estuary. It is clearly identified by its size and color. Around three to four feet tall, the adult great blue heron has a wingspan between five and six feet, making it the largest heron. The bird has a dark bluish color with a white head, and can be found around freshwater systems as well. I usually see great blue herons around the edges of marshes, sometimes camouflaged by tall grasses such as Phragmites. They get disturbed if you get too close, so walk quietly and use a pair of binoculars to see details.

Glossary

AIR BLADDER – a gas-filled structure found in rockweed which helps the plant float to the surface to maximize photosynthesis.

BYSSUS THREADS – strong fibers used by mussels to attach to an object.

CARAPACE – the outside and protective structure or shell of a crustacean.

CARNIVORE – an animal that obtains its nutrition by eating other animals.

CAUDAL FIN – the tail fin in fish.

CONIFEROUS – a tree or shrub that has cones.

DECIDUOUS – a plant that loses its leaves in the fall season.

DETRITUS – decomposing organic material that provides a food source for animals in the marsh.

DORSAL FIN – a fin located on the back of fish.

FILTER-FEEDER – an animal that obtains its nutrition by straining food substances from water.

HOLDFAST – a root-like structure in seaweeds that attaches to a substrate.

MIDRIB – a supportive structure that runs along the center of a rockweed plant.

MOLTING - the process of shedding an exoskeleton as an animal increases in size.

PANNES – pools of water in a marsh that provide habitat for many small animals.

PERENNIAL – a plant that lives for more than two years.

PLANKTON – microscopic plants and animals that drift in the water.

RADULA – a small, toothed structure in snails used for feeding.

REGENERATION – the regrowth of a structure or organ that is lost.

RHIZOME – an underground stem that can spread the growth of a plant.

SALINITY – a measure of the salt concentration in water usually in parts per thousand.

SCAVENGER – an animal that feeds on dead animal material.

SUBSTRATE – a place or object on which an organism is attached or lives.

SUCCESSION – the changes that occur in the environment over time.

SUCCULENT – a thick, fleshy plant that stores water in its tissues.

SYMBIOSIS – a relationship between two species living together that may or may not be beneficial.

URUSHIOL – the chemical found in poison ivy that causes an allergic reaction in the form of a rash.

VASCULAR PLANTS – those with specialized conducting tissues for water, minerals, and nutrients.

Recommended References

Bertness, Mark D., *The Ecology of Atlantic Shorelines*. Sinauer Associates, Inc., Sunderland, Mass. 1999.

Meinkoth, Norman A., *The Audubon Society Field Guide to North American Seashore Creatures*. Alfred A. Knopf, New York. 1981.

Sterling, Dorothy, *The Outer Lands. The American Museum Of Natural History*, New York. 1967.

Sumich, James L., *An Introduction to the Biology of Marine Life*. WCB/McGraw-Hill. 1999.

Teal, John and Mildred, *Life and Death of the Salt Marsh*. Ballantine Books, Inc. New York, NY. 1969.

Waller, Geoffrey, Ed., *Sealife – A Complete Guide to the Marine Environment*. Smithsonian Institution Press, Washington, D.C. 1996.

Acknowledgements

I am very grateful to the following individuals and organizations for their assistance in this publication:

To **Jaci Barton** and the **Barnstable Land Trust** for their strong support and commitment to conservation.

To **James R. Brown** and **Elliott G. Carr** for the use of their photographs.

To **Chris Dumas** whose excellent photographs bring out the hidden beauty of Crocker Neck.

To **Rob Gatewood** and the **Barnstable Conservation Commission** for permission to use the map, and for their stewardship of the town's wetlands and open space.

To **Diana Parker** for helping me with the text and organization of this book.

To **Nancy Viall Shoemaker** for her professional advice, suggestions, and expertise in publishing this book.

The Author

Gilbert Newton is a Cape Cod native who has been teaching environmental science at Sandwich High School and Cape Cod Community College for many years. His subjects include coastal ecology, botany, coastal zone management, and environmental technology. Gil is one of the founders of the Barnstable Land Trust and has conducted field trips to Crocker Neck for the BLT. He is also the past president of the Thornton W. Burgess Society and the Association to Preserve Cape Cod. He is the author of *Seaweeds of Cape Cod Shores*, published for the Cape Cod Museum of Natural History.

The Photographer

Chris Dumas has lived and worked on Cape Cod for over fifteen years. He currently teaches earth & space science and physics at Sandwich High School. Chris has been involved in environmental science and outdoor education for most of his career. Photography has been an important part of Chris' life for the last decade and he has travelled around the country in search of the interesting vistas. Chris has a graduate degree in Resource Conservation from the University of Montana and is a native of the St. Lawrence River Valley region of New York.

This book was designed and typeset by Nancy Viall Shoemaker of West Barnstable Press, West Barnstable, Massachusetts. The text font is Tiepolo Book, designed by Cynthia Hollandsworth of International Typeface Corporation in 1987 as a "sans serif with serifs alternative" and named after the Italian artist Dominic Tiepolo. Image credits were set in Frutiger, designed by Swiss typographer Adrian Frutiger (1928-). This font was designed in 1968 for the signage at the then-newly-built Charles De Gaulle International Airport. *The Ecology of a Cape Cod Salt Marsh* was printed on 70 lb. white opaque offset with a 12 pt. Kromekote cover.

Entire book, including cover, printed on recycled paper